THE KILN

THE KILN

Patricia V Dawson

Hub Editions

The Author: Born Patricia Vaughan Wright 1925; married James N. Dawson 1948. Patricia V. Dawson is a sculptor, printmaker and art historian. She has worked as a lecturer at the Tate Gallery, written articles on art history and criticism for various publications, booklets to accompany a series of seven slide strips entitled 'The Artist Looks at Life' (Visual Publications) and 'La Lanterne Des Morts', a poem illustrated by her own relief etchings (Ram Press).

Her etchings are in many private and public collections, including the British Museum and La Bibliotheque Nationale.

Her poems and etchings have appeared in *Brief, Borderlines, The Anglo-Welsh Review, New Welsh Review, Powys Review, The Powys Journal, Literary Review* and *Blithe Spirit.*

'The Kiln' is a selection of poems written over the last 25 years.

ISBN 1 870653 33 5

Hub Editions
11 The Ridgway
Flitwick
Bedfordshire MK45 1DH

Contents

THE KILN

THE LABYRINTH

PRIVATE VIEW

THE KILN

The kiln is open —
lift out the pots; strike each one.
Listen as it rings.

THE KILN

when we came to the Priory
the kiln was sealed;
the fire was burning
and we saw a pot
on the wheel turning.
In the cellar
barrels were sleeping
and in the Chapter House
pillars leaping.
across the courtyard
two pigeons flying
and on the ground
two pigeons dying
from one cartridge
and Jean Marc shooting.
Their blood was as red
as the wine we were drinking
but not as bright
as the logs that were burning.
Behold a plume
from the chimney smoking—
when I said, "The Vatican,"
I was joking.

PARENTS VISITING

Whether in the suburbs
or a country town,
you can always spot them,
at Christmas or in June,
out for a walk,
keeping discreet intervals
between getting under foot.

Tact is implicit in their clothes,
generally new and carefully chosen.
They walk in the street,
sometimes with a grandchild
who runs ahead
towards the traffic.
Hoping he'll stop in time
(they could not catch him
if they tried)
they trust to fate.

They sigh for occupation,
remembering how only yesterday
they hurried to the shops,
the school, the dentist
and a thousand crises.
Now they mark time,
glad that they're not besieged,
flooded, or blown up,
or anything else
that they read in the papers.

THREE WOMEN

One craves occupation.
Two needs praise
and Three survives on grit
while One will sit and knit
and Two prefers to pose.

One travels just to say she's been.
Two travels to enrich her image
and Three travels far
to see relations,
people she has never met,
in boring places.

One has settled for a role,
subservient to her man
and stereotypes him.
Two looks to men as comforters
and Three, though married,
wipes them from her mind
expecting nothing.

One had no aspirations.
She has found
that looking forward is the way
and Two survives in hope
of finding someone
who will understand.
Three had abandoned hope
though very long ago
she had her dreams,
she's learnt to live
with disappointment.

Round they go,
marking each season
with an extra line.
One goes blueish grey
where Two prefers to tint
and Three forgets the colour of her hair.

VENICE JULY 1971

There is a Venetian lady
who walks every evening
towards the Piazzale Roma
to meet her husband.
He works on the mainland,
probably at Mestre.
That is why she walks every evening
at the same time
to meet him at the car park.

She is a little bit like
Marilyn Monroe and Elizabeth Taylor
and all Hollywood
as she walks to the car park
with her hair carefully set
and her dress carefully pressed
and her half smile
carefully applied.

She is anxious during the day,
when he is on the mainland.
She worries about him
as she shops in the market
in the early morning.
And most of all
she worries in the afternoon
when she lies on her bed
and tries to sleep.

He works in an air conditioned office.
In the next room there are two typists,
one is dark and the other fair
and they giggle and type;
and she has no children,
no small, dark, Venetian children.
That is why she
can walk in the evening
to meet her husband
when he comes to the car park.

She has met her husband.
He kisses her in the Piazzale Roma,
among the coaches and the tourists,
among the stalls of cheap souvenirs
and the distracted couriers
and the confident porters;
and they walk beside the canal,
arm in arm.
She is Elizabeth Taylor
and Marilyn Monroe
and the reflections of the buildings
smile up at them
through the water.
This is another evening
when he has come back to her from the mainland
and for a moment she has no more fear.

THE LAST TIGER

(for R.S.Thomas)

Once preserved by Moguls
for hunting,
the last tiger sits moping
in his cage.
Mateless, he has nowhere to go.

Sometimes he is drawn
on a trailer
in processions.
Idealists tried to save him
but he defied
their benevolence
by eating their cattle.

His roar echoes
through a world
no longer hungry
for his language.

He speaks to them
of a past that they
prefer to forget
and a future
that will never occur.

CUL DE SAC

They invented a religion.
Stone was power.
Earth was wisdom.
Water was foolishness.

They built a temple of stone,
planted a garden in the earth,
but without water
nothing would grow.

THE WHITE PHEASANT

(a story told of an Earl of Powys)

Among the trees
and gentle prospects
strutted a white bird,
his lordship's pheasant,
by nature selected,
by his command protected.
Season after season
he rose with the others
when the beaters
crashed through the bracken.

The guns knew not to shoot
this freak
that whirred
aloft and landed
safe but deserted,
until, one day, a stranger
to the story
aimed from the shoulder.
Ignorance had made him bolder
than the rest.
"A white pheasant, great,
I'll shoot him."

There he lay, alone,
retrieved by a panting dog,
beside the others,
heaped for market.
No one dared touch
his Lordship's pheasant,
a Moby Dick, stranded,
waiting for Captain Ahab
who never claimed him.

His Lordship preferred
this pheasant live.
Dead he was not for eating.
The thoughtless guest
was never asked again.

REPLACING THE HANGINGS ON NELSON'S HAMMOCK

A wooden cradle
swings in The Victory
in the hero's cabin.
It had delicate hanging
embroidered by his 'D
Half whore, half godde
she worked a magic ne
drawn threadwork for
and then flowers twinin
on pale silk for Nelson.
Having outlived him, t
perishing in a museum,
three ladies, as stout as
sit in his cabin
repeating a pattern
as the little hammock
swings gently from a b

P.4 a blush grey
P.73 caused 2 Errata
There are 2 more P.(6)

A FRIENDLY MESSIAH

(Swift at first refused to allow
the choir and musicians of
St Patrick's Cathedral to sing
in the first performance of
The Messiah in Dublin in 1742)

Oh Swift!
in what mood tyrannical
could you have bade
your choir
and your musicians
eschew the Master's work?
Handel, your equal
in another art,
in Dublin, and you not part
of his great night.

Having bowed
to diplomatic wiles
you let them go.
Could you then resist
creeping with Stella's
hoopless ghost
into the crowded hall,
at the back perhaps?

Gentlemen were asked
to leave their swords at home.
You, in clerical attire
were swordless anyhow.
Did your hand reach
towards her in the crush?

— a burst of trumpets
and behold two stars
in one great Hallelujah.

(Note: Due to the cramped space
in a crowded room, gentlemen were
requested to leave their swords at
home and ladies their hoops. Stella
died in 1728)

EPITAPH

Robins are reckless;
fly too near,
show no fear.

This one intruded
but we bore the draught from his wings
on our faces;
imagined him a messenger,
of a death perhaps,
and now we know
it was his own.

THE MYTHRAKERS

(A protest at the serialisation in
The Sunday Times in the '70's of
revelations of T.E.Lawrence's
private life)

Lawrence or Arthur,
how we need heroes who reflect ourselves.
We long to chat to Arthur's concubines
and find at Cadbury his seraglio.
New myths are easier to scar,
nearer than Camelot is Aqaba.
Icarus fell to justify our lusts,
so when the mythrakers melt the wax,
we say,
"Who's for whipping this fine sabbath day?"

THREE SELF PORTRAITS

The Magus

When young I played at being old,
then old at being young,
a tongue in cheek hide and seek
of my own making.

Charts predict my progress
from set to set
and the backdrop rattles
in the draught from the window.

Sunlight is trying to get in
But I prefer to wield my pen
under the anglepoise.
I have rejected magic
for a papier mâché world.

The Scold

There are no mirrors in my house.
I cannot see my face;
I have been wronged
but I shall not be bridled.
My pots and pans are clean
and there are roses round the door,

but oh how it slams
when I go out and in
and how the sound of the Furies
rings in my ears
as I try to rest.
Turn up the sound;
I shall not sleep
until I find redress.

The Prophet

I have no belongings;
they would impede me
as I climb the mountain.
I go up there every day
and shout my prophecies
to the wind.
The wind carries them
across the sea,
but when they reach land
they are unintelligible.
Hear me, oh wind!
Hear me, oh waves!
Unscramble my prophecies
I must descend to eat;
it is lunch time
and the ravens are on strike.

MINUTIAE

Let us concentrate on details,
dotting the ‘i’’s and crossing the ‘t’’s,
polishing the doorknob for the thousandth time.
Let us look through the microscope
at infinitesimal things,
bacteria, chromosomes,
so that we may plumb the source of life.
Let us be diverted
by hair-splitting arguments
beguiled by tautology,
pinned down by balancing angels.
Let us be diverted by small things,
the cry of a baby,
or a twinge of pain,
for they are all blessings
and shut out the cold.

THE OWL BOX

"We liked the sound of the owls,"
she said.
The owl box had arrived
to be fixed to the barn,
but within a week
they were going to live
in a suburb,
semi-detached and safe;
too old for the house
up the lane.
It had come too late.

The white sweeping of wings
would be seen by other eyes
and the ghostly cry
would be heard by other ears,
not by them in their own
new box;
but perhaps in the night
a remembered sound
will soothe their fears
and a nesting
will happen beside the walnut tree
in the new owl box.

ON SEEING THE DUKE OF WINDSOR ON TELEVISION

He sits in his place in the Bois,
a modern king,
sing honi soit.
He tried to help the unemployed,
a charity kings should avoid.
Instead of being crowned with thanks,
he found that he had joined their ranks.
A modern king cannot advance;
he must retreat,
lest mal y pense.

THE DUKE OF WINDSOR: AN EPITAPH

Much decorated
and often painted,
he waited,
halted in his tracks.
He was the man who failed
to paper over the cracks.

ON RE-READING 'MAIDEN CASTLE'

The puppet master's gone
blown by a ghost wind on the sea.
By lighting fires in dewponds
he could make his puppets weep.
The strings are cut
and they are left to laugh and lech
beside the scummy pond
or wander anxious on the Icen Way.
Tell them he's coming back;
Quirm's wooden bowl
is always full of elderberry wine
and they shall drink
together for the thousandth time.

'Maiden Castle' — a novel by John Cowper Powys

CITIZENS OF THE WORLD

Is it possible for them
to kick the habit of a national costume?
Is it easy to pull down the flag
and, having done so,
must they live in a perpetual sundown?

They must pack their bags
and move on.
He looks like Captain Ahab
and comes from the same root.
She like Isadora
and how she travelled!

They have children
and they have money,
but they have no home.
They search for the edge of the world
and vacillate
between two poles:
Nordic mercy
and the ruthless peace of Zen.

When will they be still?
The grass will not
grow under their feet,
but, one day,
it will grow over them.

THE DREAMING TIME

The old man cries before he goes to sleep.
He has no heirs to help him on his way,
no one who knows the sacred words to say,
no one to climb the rocks and speak
to guardian spirits,
fathers of this world.

Eagles and crocodiles preside below;
one man remains
who paints them with a twig.
Earth colours glow on bark.
A snow of white is spewed
around a stencilled hand.

The spirits fade.
No one will climb the rocks
to ask for help.
The cave of bones remains,
but out of reach.
The old man dies before he goes to sleep.

(Note: The old man is one of a few remaining members
of a dwindling tribe of Australian Aborigines.
The Dreaming Time is the world in which their spirits
live before they are born and to which they return
at death. The cave of bones is an ossuary belonging
to the tribe.)

SHADOWS

There's a club for the people
with plastic surgery faces.
There's a pub for the heroes
who tunnelled under the wire;
but where do the shadows meet
who wandered in the wilderness
while others warmed their hands
at the nursery fire?

They hide their cold faces in masks of iron.
They shield their bodies in cloaks of steel.
Some of them climb to high places
to see what the endless horizons
might reveal.

Some of them call from ivory towers.
Some of them weep in solitary valleys.
Some of them search for companions in the night
in raucous, fun filled alleys.

All of them are alone,
but sometimes a mask falls
and one frightened face
smiles at another.
As the two faces meet
each recalls
a non-existent mother.

PHEASANTS

In June a few fine pheasants
look for grain
on a green lawn,
tails criss-crossing,
beaks pecking
at grass mowings
thrown by little girls cheating.

In August men are shooting,
woods across the valley exploding,
beaters beating,
pheasants retreating
in dozens
to the green lawn,
death cheating.

COTSWOLD WEDDING

The morning's cold, the supermarket's bright
And packs of shoppers hurry through the streets.
A-hunting we will go.

The eager car attacks the motorway
and joins the field which canters down the lanes.
Fog is expected and the signals warn.
The anxious driver's crouching at the wheel.
A-hunting we will go.

The bells are ringing from the ancient tower.
The bellringers have got their sweaters on.
Their breath creates a mist inside the church
and all the congregation hustles in.
A-hunting we will go.

The valley's cold, the cottages are bleak
and winter has obscured the picturesque.
Man has attempted to redress the fault
and horseback hunters trot among the fields.
A-hunting we will go.

Tears prick our eyelids as we sit and wait,
Split down the middle for the bride and groom.
Don't get entangled is a backward glance;
it's sharpened to destroy the other side.
A-hunting we will go.

Husband adheres to wife and child to child,
infinite feeling in a little time.
The vicar's smooth, the stone heads watch the show,
their eyes betray a dignified concern.
The singing warms the hollows in the roof
and ricochets against the wooden beams.
This noise denies the element of spoof
and for an instant life is what it seems.
A-hunting we will go.

Champagne and cake entice us to the fire
and cruelty and cold are far away.
The compliments and jealousies are aired
and in this atmosphere the two are one.
Behold the bride and groom are gone away
leaving the followers who watched the fun.
A-hunting we will go

VERY LIKE AN ISLAND?

There were these monks
who went on a voyage
in a leather boat
across the Atlantic.
"Mad!" I hear you say,
but that's life —
mad every inch of the way.

They were tired and cramped
and then, what luck,
they found an island.
They pulled in and got out
to stretch their legs.
They were thirsty
with all that work
and the salt spray
so they made a fire
and brewed up.
Just as they were enjoying themselves,
one of them noticed
that the island had begun to move.

"Help!" they cried
and scrambled
back into the boat.

Meanwhile the island gathered speed
and disappeared over the horizon
with the fire still burning on its back.

"Its back?" I hear you say.
Yes, it was a whale.

If I'd been there,
I would have seen that
from the first.
I would have stayed in the boat,
midst much derision.

What I want to know is —
when are you going to realise
that you are sitting on a whale?

AN UNCIVIL WAR
(THE ETERNAL QUARREL)

"Let's play Cavaliers and Roundheads.
Bags I'm a Cavalier
and you're a Roundhead, dear.
I shall wear feathers and ribbons
and I shall be there
reminding you of all the things you fear."

"Oh no, you won't, I'll have none of them.
My world's a world of words;
my theories stem from absolutes.
I drink the whey and throw away the curds —
they're dross. You wallow in the cream
and pullulate in an erroneous dream.
None of your illusions are what they seem.
I am the bedrock of reality:
I see life whole, a true totality.
Let's make a treaty and I will not pass
the boundary of your ever farting arse.
Once I was strong by calling on the Lord;
that was luxury that now I can't afford,
but I remain yours TRULY
in this campaign.

"Oh no, you don't. The players have arrived;
the theatre's open and the crowds throng in.
It gives them joy. They're laughing
as a young maid plays a boy.
You tell them that these fripperies must go,
but they know better
for these things were ever so
and from these fantasies
realities will grow.
At my sword point, in you go."

AN OPEN DAY
AT THE PHYSIC GARDEN

Caged wheat and no birds;
there are only people in the garden —
people looking at herbs.
The sun rides a dragon
through the garden
under the mulberry trees
and withered pods incline their faces,
touching the earth which is raked and weeded,
making sure that nothing has seeded
that isn't labelled or needed.
The leaves change colour
and flowers are noted
under the air where the dragon floated.
A stone man and no birds.
There are only people in the garden —
people looking at trees.

THE LITTLE CHRISTMAS

Today is Sunday.
It is Twelfth Night.
Tomorrow will be Little Christmas.

Three bowed figures in raincoats,
pensioners to a man,
struggle up hill
against the wind,
carrying plastic Christmas trees,
dismantled decorations.
No corporation lorry or young men
work today,
but bad luck must be averted.

One carries his on his head,
African style,
the others at their sides.
They are taking away bedraggled offerings,
three wise men,
conceived by Stanley Spencer
against a background of red brick.

As Birnam to Dunsinane,
so Cookham came to Ludlow.

(Note: The Little Christmas is the Irish name for January 6th, the date of Christmas on the Julian Calendar still celebrated in England until 1752.)

TWO GARDENERS

First

Off with their heads.
Their colour does not match my scheme.
This garden is all white,
a Midsummer Night's Dream,
virginal, despite
a tendency to blight.
Bring out the spray
and we'll put that to flight.

Second

I've planted wild flowers,
stolen from the fields;
they're spreading on the lawn:
we cannot mow.
The traveller's joy has rioted and now
in autumn covers everything like snow.
The sweet briar rambles,
don't you love the smell?
The elecampane's blooming in the glade;
we fetch our water from an ancient well;
the newts are rampant in that pond we made.

First

How can you let those weeds choke up the beds?
And all your columbines are wild and blue.
You must be going crazy in the head
to let the general public in to view.
I must be getting back; oh what a pest,
the roses that I planted by the wall
are pink, a shade I heartily detest —
I plan to get a brush and paint them all.

SIGHT SEEING

Ludlow is a must for solitary ladies.
They trudge purposefully
from street to street,
some with cameras,
all with sensibly shod feet,
absorbed by buildings,
amazed at 'black and white'
and Georgian vistas.

They peer through spectacles;
no smile escapes their lips;
hoping that tea
will wash away their loneliness,
they make a bargain with a now
that promises a memory,
carefully preserved,
of happiness when they were here.

THE FUR COAT

The model had been posing
naked, on a cold morning.
As she rested, warming herself
with a cup of tea, she told me
about a fur coat,
bought second hand
by her sister-in-law.
It has a silk lining,
embroidered with summer flowers,
hollyhocks and delphiniums,
turning the seasons
inside out.

THE LABYRINTH

THE LABYRINTH
Scenes from an Autobiographical Journey

Ariadne

"Cape hoc linum," she said
as she handed Theseus a ball of red wool.
We acted on a green bank
in the school garden.

Polyphemus (The ophthalmologist)

"Out of the grave," he roared as he grasped my hand.
Then he looked through one shining eye
into mine and deplored
my poor circulation.
"Better or worse?" he growled
as he turned his lenses.

Socrates (A teacher)

"It was a whirlwind courtship,"
he said as he remembered two lovers.
"I am going to leave like a shot from a gun,"
he announced, as he took down his coat.
But he is here,

looking over my shoulder.
"When in doubt, use black,"
he advised and I do,
in mourning for his youth.

Lamri (A bride)

She must tread the bridal path.
Insert the bit.
Snaffled and curbed, she will
trot between hedges.
She is not yet broken.
When she foals,
she will stand patient beside her young.
Out to grass she will be remembered
with a lump of sugar
and later by a name over the stable door:
GIPSY.

Daedalus (A sculptor)

"Let's cheat a bit," he said
as he sidled from studio to studio
off a dark passage

in a haze of cologne.
Icarus was an American airman.

Chronos (A grandfather)

"Remember," he said,
"When I am dead, 'Two wrongs
don't make a right.'"
And I do and they don't.

The Light

The white walls of the labyrinth
are stained with rainbows;
the light rises from the ground
through the body
to the head.

The Darkness

The Darkness stalks where there is light.
It chants potent gibberish
in a monotone
and knows no rest.

Orpheus (A poet)

"Has anyone got a poim?" he said,
between two gulps of beer.
"If they haven't, I've got one here."
And out of his pocket he drew
an edited part of his life
on a wafer of paper.
Now he's put down his pen
and his beer and deserted his wife,
but I wish he was here.

Lachesis (A healer)

"It's a virus," she says
as she picks up the phone.
"It will last seven days,
after that who can say?
Let me know if it doesn't go away."
And she turns to her weaving.
She hasn't a choice.
Nobody heard her voice
when they ordered the pattern:
she is left with the thread
that links the living with the dead.

The Centre

At the centre
there is a tunnel.
At the end of the tunnel,
a bright landscape,
still and empty.

At the centre there is a tunnel.
At the end of the tunnel
there is a room that changes.
Sometimes the walls are hung
with curious objects.
At other times there is an empty bed
with tossed sheets.
At the end of the tunnel there is no time.

ON AN OYSTER SHELL

(Found among the excavations of
a Roman Villa in Dorchester in 1938)

It was evacuation
and Munich time
and we drove over
from Somerset,
school uniformed.
We, who were used
to shivering
beside open fires
marvelled at the remains
of central heating.

I stooped to pick up
an oyster shell,
coated with white powder,
flaking at the edges.
I shuffled round
muddy trenches
half listening
to the guide,
half looking at the sky
as I fingered
the pilfered shell
in my raincoat pocket,
snug as the piece of paper
Chamberlain waved.

We came home to London
reprieved from war,
only to return
the next year
to Somerset,
to fear an invasion
that might have brought
central heating
and, who knows,
another oyster shell?

MY MATERNAL GRANDFATHER

He could cure hiccups.
Together we would breathe in
deeply and then slowly
let it go.

He could catch trout.
He taught me to cast
a fly with a small green apple
at the end of a string
tied to a cane.

He grew roses,
forked them neatly,
pruned nearly down to the ground,
well ordered and labelled,
Mrs McCready and Daily Mail,
Paul Birt and Independence Day.

He could click his thumb,
sing Ho Jolly Jenkin
and tell tales of a trip
to the Argentine.

He endured the Blitz
with his hat on
in the cellar
and died forty five years ago
unsure of where he was going.

JASPER

A stone, a Magus and a child
who looks into the past,
the future
and the present day.

A blackhaired Janus
comes into the world
that looks both ways,
follows a star,
casts a stone,
searches for a Magus
and finds a child.

(Note: Jasper is a grandchild
born on January 2nd 1992)

THE CAPTIVE

She is an odalisque
Walking on tiptoe to please
her master.
She is a conjurer
using sleight of hand
to find coins in our ears.
She is the conjuror's
accomplice blinding
the audience
with her shapely legs.
She is a dwarf
that runs errands.
She is a medium
calling up the future
and obliterating the past.
She wraps it in a cloud
and hides it behind the sofa.
She brings in the drinks
clutching the tray
as if her life depended on it
because she is drowning,
drowning in the past,
drowning in the future.
Her feet have left the sand
and the lifebelts
are under the hatches.

The waves will break
over her and muffle
her cries.
That is why
she must walk on tiptoe
to please her master.

DOING BACK CRAWL WITH TOBY

We started off across the pool.
Two seals, we swam
in unison, divided
by sixty years
and only a foot or two of water.

We puffed and blew,
I rather more than he and we smiled as we
reached the other side,
one seal of approval.

THE ECLIPSE OF THE MOON

If I were Poet Laureate
I should write a poem
about the Eclipse of the Moon
and note that the Palace
chose that day,
December the ninth nineteen ninety two,
to announce the separation of the Waleses.

If I were Poet Laureate
I should recall the abdication
of Edward the Eighth,
how, on the night
of December the eleventh nineteen thirty six,
I went to a performance
of The Yeoman of the Guard
and I shivered as I sang
God Save the King
because I sang for George the Sixth.

But I am not Poet Laureate
so I cannot point out
that the Palace has chosen
an appropriate day
to make their announcement,
Diana being the Goddess of the Moon,
and I did not see the eclipse
because of low cloud.

THE TOY COOKER

I remember it now,
a small shining replica
six by six by six.
There were saucepans
and a frying pan,
built to scale.
I planned tiny meals for dolls.

To power it there was
a spirit burner:
"Too dangerous," I was told.
I abandoned hopes
of minute fry ups,
little choppings of real veg
for boiling. Instead
I tore up coloured paper.
Imagination, strained
to its limits, evaporated
and the little cooker
stayed in the toy cupboard.

Now I stand beside
a grown up one
and cook for real.
Living more and more in the head,
perhaps one day I shall pretend
again with shredded paper,
served up like phoney money
at a Chinese funeral.

BUTTERFLY

I am a butterfly
caught in the net
of your imitation weakness.
I am a caterpillar
squashed under your heel.
I am the pain of humiliation
that you suffered
but dare not feel.

HUNTRESS

How was the chase
and was the killing sweet?
I hope so
because now you sit
surrounded by the carcasses
you cannot eat.

IN SEARCH OF A DEAD FATHER

I

Perhaps I'd find him in that room in the basement,
among the trunks.
A Union Jack lay on the table
as it must have lain on his coffin.
A black tin box contained his uniform,
his sporran and his skean-dhu.
Was this the one he used
to kill a German sniper
bold enough to stalk him
in No Man's Land?
Since that time he could not bear
anyone to walk behind him.
If I followed
would I confront that knife raised
to send me back to life?
He joined that German.
Do they talk of old times?
I would have been de trop.
Hand to hand fighting did not suit my mood.
I searched for comfort and I found a gap.

II

There was a road down which I never walked.
There was a vocie to which I never talked.
There was a hand that I never held.

There was a tree that is destroyed and felled.
There was a face at which I never smiled.
There was a father and here is a child.

There were two eyes at which I never laughed.
There was a mouth by which I was not chaffed.
There were two lips by which I was not kissed.
There was a heart by which I was not missed.

There was a body that's well and truly dead.
There is a soul that's well and truly fled.
There are the memories that others had.
They are the shadowing that makes me sad.

There was anger that I could not fear.
There was comfort that was not near.
There was sorrow that I could not bear.
There was triumph that I could not share.
Here are the tears which I could never shed.
Silent they wait imprisoned in my head.

(Note: Theodore James Wright, a professional soldier, commissioned in the Seaforth Highlanders, served with the Royal Flying Corps in the First World War. He was killed while flying a plane on manoeuvres in 1927.)

WATER

They called me up the lane
to see the pump,
shining black in a clearing,
newly painted,
put right:
it works.
Andrew cranks the handle
and, just as we give up,
the brown water comes
and falls on the dried earth.
Above, hanging trees
cling to an old quarry,
their canopy of branches interlaced;
brambles curl round our feet.
Will the water clear?
Is it ground water
or a muddied spring?
Clarity is what we need
to explain, baptise
and wash away our tears,
comfort and contain.
But it runs away
and soaks the earth,
leaving questions unanswered
while we pump and strain.

THE FLAX FIELD

I stood beside the flax field
and watched the wind
blow criss-cross currents
through a tawny sea.
One blue flower
was shining at the edge.

I had not looked at flax
since, over forty years before,
I'd pulled it, in a gang.
We strained shoulder to shoulder,
dragging it from the earth,
our eyes and noses pouring from the dust.

I listened to the wind among the stalks.
The sound was like a whispered tinnitus,
reminding me of other years
and other harvests
watered by more painful tears.

EDUCATION

When Tabitha was tested
for her school,
they made her draw
(as usual art corralled
by education)
a figure.

"Did she draw the fingers?"
asked a knowall friend.
"That's the way they do it —
measure four year olds."

Her mother wondered.
Tabitha piped up
"I didn't give her any arms."
Oh dear,
the family is gripped by fear.
Perhaps she will not make the grade.
Even Tabitha is quite afraid.

How much education does it take
to give a thought to William Blake?
Schoolless, he roamed the fields.
Politically brave,
he wrote and drew his life away
and, better still,
went singing to his grave.

MIDWIFE

I have tried forceps,
love and tears.
Come out, for God's sake,
scramble through the hole.
Yes, you are camouflaged,
but in clothing that you chose.

Raise your voice,
scream as you come in
and dress in your true colours,
if you know their name.
Others have coaxed you
all in vain,
only to be savaged.
They lick their wounds and slink away.
Only I remain,
but daunted and quite numb with pain.

CATTLE CROSSING

"Are there any animals
where we are going?" she asked,
hoping for a friendly cat
at a boring destination.
"No," I said, but I was wrong.
When we had climbed Dorstone Hill,
there at the top were cattle,
not just cows on the way
to be milked, or calves to be earmarked,
or heifers to be taken to market,
but all of these,
pouring out of a field on to the road,
facing in all directions;
dun calves caked in mud,
black and white cows,
clustered heifers, trotting in unison.
And I stopped the car.

"I hope there's a man with them,"
she said and at last
we heard a voice. It said,
"Hoi, hoi!" and I breathed more slowly.
We sat and waited.
Then I inched forward
into a welcome gap,
but still they came, which way

he intended it was hard to tell.
Sometimes they followed him,
sometimes they turned back.
Eventually we crawled through the crowd
and found him smiling.
He waved both arms
and I saluted with a thankful grin.

"There were your animals," I said.
"Shall we go home the other way?"
she suggested.

MOTHERHOOD

I always swore
that I would never
write a wombic poem.
Now they've flown
I run an airport
duty free.
The planes touch down
and then take off again,
leaving me
caught in the slipstream
symbolising what?
A breast, an anchor, or a key?

PARTING

The train leaves like a tide receding.
My body stands like a hacked tree bleeding.
My body moves like a robot walking.
My voice speaks like a megaphone talking.
The air is cold like a winding sheet freezing.
The car is enclosed like a womb teasing.

The roads are oblivious of where I am going
the people on them a crowd of unknowing.
My destination is full of weeping,
but the shred that is left will wake from sleeping.

HEIRLOOMS

What shall we take from the house?
Practical things,
talismans for survival.
A duster,
a tape measure,
a hoover and an iron.

Leave the Chippendale chairs
and the Georgian silver
that clogged each mouthful.
I faced severance from these
and they let go.

Let the dealers come in
and put values on them
different from those I knew.
There is no fear in a cold cheque,
no emotional tie.
Let it buy
taxis and parking space
and freedom.

A TYRESOME STORY

My paternal grandfather
was very proud of the fact
that, when he was a young curate
in Belfast, he had known Dr Dunlop,
the inventor of
the inflatable rubber tyre.

It appears that Dr Dunlop's son
had a bicycle
and for whatever reason,
it had shed what bicycles had
in those days –
its solid rubber tyres.

How this had happened
I could never understand.
I had had solid
rubber tyres on my fairy cycle
and they had never shown signs
of wear and tear.

However, this to young Dunlop's bike
had obviously happened
and his father, being a man
of infinite resources,

went into his surgery
where he found two rubber tubes.
These he blew up and sealed,
having at first, presumably,
wrapped them round Dunlop junior's
bike's bare rims — oh joy —
making young Dunlop the very first boy
to ride on air.

Very many men of God,
I have noticed, are obsessed
by wheeled vehicles
and my grandfather was no exception.
It was only a matter of minutes before he died
that he had dismounted from his bicycle.

PRIVATE VIEW

FIGURATIVE ART

Ere Jackson Pollock poured his paint
and Manet cause Eugenie's fainting,
two copulated sans restraint
and Man was man's first action painting.

THE RODIN EXHIBITION AT THE HAYWARD GALLERY

Trapped in concrete the figures writhe,
flesh turned to clay
and clay to bronze.
Up the spiral stair we go,
clutching our catalogues to the Gates of Hell.
The bodies leap and lie
and kiss and cringe.
Below, the portrait busts
stare at each other:
Clemenceau
and Bernard Shaw;
a proustean countess lifts her head.
Balzac swaggers nude,
or stands, swaying slightly,
in his dressing gown.
Flesh was his medium
and here it is,
with all its power and pain.

NOVEMBER IN THE MUSEE RODIN or RODIN CHEZ LUI

It is cold in the Champ de Mars.
The Seine has given up her dead
to an elegant morgue.
A centauress stretches towards a tree
from marble haunches.
Our loins are petrified
as we stare through the windows
at red roses,
shrivelled lips
guarding a fossil house.

FOR CAMILLE CLAUDEL

Cut these shrunken winter roses;
lay them like straw in the street.
In their bruising we shall feel her grief.

Behold Les Bavardes
who meet
in a green corner of Parnassus.
Naked they tell how it was
to love a colossus.

(Note: Les Bavardes, a sculpture, made of
green onyx and bronze, of nude figures
gossiping at a table in the corner of a room.

Camille Claudel who sculpted it was in love
with Rodin. Rejected by him, she was confined to
a mental asylum for the last thirty years
of her life.)

MATISSE'S SNAIL: WHEN THE ROOF LEAKED AT THE TATE

My master lay in bed
and cut me out,
marked my shape
with charcoal on a stick
and I was stuck on,
a geometric whirligig.

Now the rain is coming in.
I never saw rain,
never slid
like other snails
over wet ground;
never explored rocks and bricks.
I got my kicks
here in the dry
from the admiration of passers by.
Common snails move slowly,
        but I shall run and run.

JACOB AND THE ANGEL
BY JACOB EPSTEIN
(On loan to the Tate Gallery)

Lord how they wrestle here
amidst dismay.
Gill's timid groupings, pale grey,
shrink before the tempest.
Passers by, intent on other things,
pursue their way,
hellbent for 'Heritage'.
They find Jacobean men,
prim in their conviction
that all was well,
backed by their neat estates,
well hedged and walled,
they contemplate globes
and gardens
and sniff at new imported fruits,
eager for exploration.

These two stand,
one shorthaired,
the other with crimped tresses,
in a terrible turmoil
of inextricable mating.
The brown alabaster
glows from the heat.
No bell is rung,
no referee cries halt
and we do not know the score

THE BUST OF A CHILD IN THE MUSEE CALVET AVIGNON

In the street pimps sidle softly;
in the courtyard peacocks peck delicately
and in the museum tourists trail
                    silently over the cool floor.

This child is white with gilded hair,
intensely grave with unspoken knowledge,
looking inwards,
young yet experienced with Time.

His neck has been broken and mended;
here chronology is upended:
his origin is uncertain
but his presence is as incisive as a knife.

We are poised on the brink of compassion
while in the street the pimps sidle softly
and in the courtyard the peacocks peck delicately
and in the museum the tourists trail
                    silently over the cool floor.

HUBRIS

When I admired her Bolivian rug,
which at a distance
could be compared to
wind blowing
over the pampas
and where I could detect
a regiment of rearing serpents,
she pointed out
a mistake in the pattern.

"Look," she said,
"It is there
in the third row from the left,"
but I knew that it was the weaver's
little sacrifice to the gods.

ON NOT CROSSING THE BRIDGE AT GIVERNY

"Have you been to Giverny?"
she asked,
brandishing the Monet cookbook.
"It's all there."
She had found her quarry,
had had her brief affair
with beauty,
eaten her fill,
experienced a thrill.
There was no more to tell,
but I must go to Giverny.

Irises were what I thought of:
an oblong painting
in Trafalgar Square
by a master chef.
Proustwise I recalled the taste.
I had been to Giverny.

(Note: Claude Monet created a garden at Giverny in order to paint it.)

AUCTION

Vincent Van Gogh
come blow up your horn.
The wolf's in the meadow,
the crow's in the corn.

Where is the man
that made this gold?
He's under the hammer
and under the mould.

L.S.LOWRY

I met him at the Tate,
a dark lumbering shape
with a tapering head
against a white ground.

He has blotted up
the life around,
dark shapes
against a white ground.
Alone he walks in the street
or sits by the sea,
direct and profound,
a dark shape
against a white ground.

AN EPITAPH FOR KURT SCHWITTERS

We walk over the silent carpet. He was poor.
It is warm. He was cold.
The telephone purrs.
The director of the gallery answers.
His voice is made of silk.

"Yes, it's sad," he says,
"So sad:
he died too soon after the war;
we could not promote him.
He was at Ambleside.
His Merzbild has been taken to Newcastle.
The farmer wanted to pull down the barn.
How much is number 33?
Number 33 is two thousand."

The spent tickets and the cellophane
add up to this?
Not a golden handshake
but a pinchbeck kiss.

THE BALLAD OF STANLEY SPENCER

In Cookham Town was born a man
for whom the Lord devised a plan.
He set him drawing his whole life's span
and his name was Stanley Spencer.

When he grew up to be sixteen,
he came to London where he'd not been
but not to see the King and Queen —
they didn't know Stanley Spencer.

He painted here and he painted there,
but most he painted in Cookham, where
the Lord inspired a love affair
twixt Cookham and Stanley Spencer.

He married once, he married twice.
He thought two wives would add some spice,
but neither of them thought it was nice,
so both left Stanley Spencer.

He painted the Resurrection Day
with all his friends in artless play
whiling the radiant time away
with God and Stanley Spencer.

Nevertheless he made the scene;
he came to London to see the Queen;
she raised him higher than he had been:
he became Sir Stanley Spencer.

We'll sing a song of the artist's life:
a lot of it's trouble,
a lot of it's strife.
You can't cut ice with a palette knife
and neither could Stanley Spencer.

The books come out and the money comes in,
but he's away from the noise and din.
It's Cookham churchyard they buried him in.
Three cheers for Stanley Spencer.

THE WORKING HORSE

(A piece of sculpture in Walsall)

Made from nuts and bolts,
ropes and buckles,
cast in bronze,
it was built from
the detritus of local history.

Expendable, it met
with a logical end,
vandalised by the grandchildren
of those it memorialised.

PORTRAIT OF TITUS

(By Rembrandt in Dulwich Gallery)

He looks into my soul
ready to strike
each surface that his eyes explore.
He looks for more and more;
it hurts.
I must close my eyes.
He needs them open.
What can I see
that the Tarot has not shown?
A textured planet
that reflects the shape of gods
and their devices.
I must search the unknown
so that one day
all who look at me
will say,
"Here is a young man
who was too vulnerable."

(Note: Titus was Rembrandt's only son
who died aged 26.)

Hand Made
In
A Garden Shed
In
Bunyan Land